DACHSHUNDS

FAVORITE DOG BREEDS

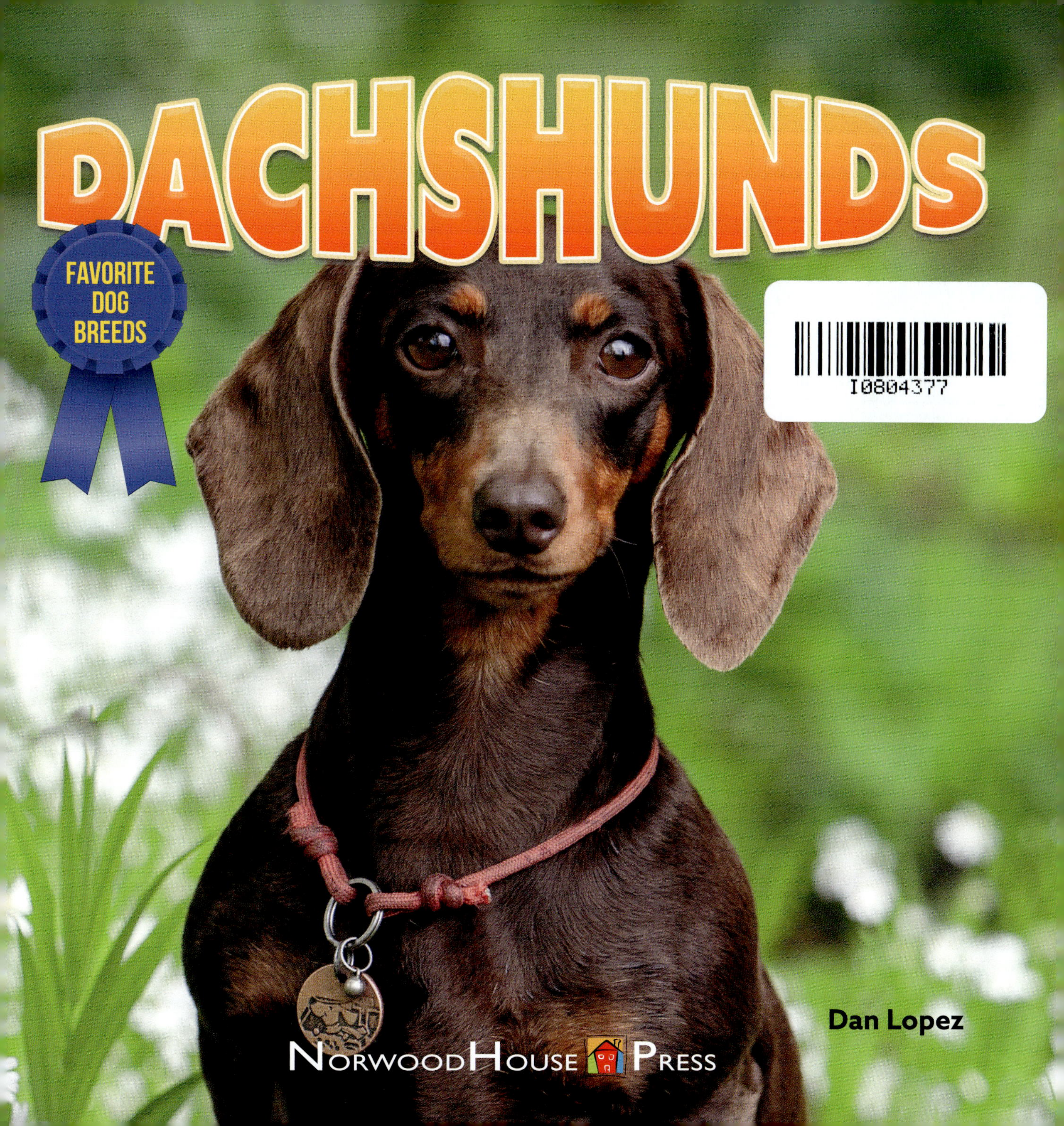

Dan Lopez

NORWOOD HOUSE PRESS

Cataloging-in-Publication Data

Names: Lopez, Dan.
Title: Dachshunds / Dan Lopez.
Description: Buffalo, NY : Norwood House Press, 2026. | Series: Favorite dog breeds| Includes glossary and index.
Identifiers: ISBN 9781978576681 (pbk.) | ISBN 9781978576698 (library bound) | ISBN 9781978576704 (ebook)
Subjects: LCSH: Dachshunds--Juvenile literature.
Classification: LCC SF429.D25 L67 2026 | DDC 636.7538--dc23

Published in 2026 by
Norwood House Press
2544 Clinton Street
Buffalo, NY 14224

Designer: Rhea Magaro
Editor: Kim Thompson

Photo credits: Cover, p. 1 Shedara Weinsberg, Giraphics/Shutterstock.com; p. 4 Soho A Studio/Shutterstock.com; p. 5 asturfauna/Shutterstock.com; p. 6 otsphoto/Shutterstock.com; p. 7 Tammy27/Shutterstock.com; p. 8 James Player/Shutterstock.com; p. 9 Anna Pozzi - Zoophotos/Shutterstock.com; p. 10 KseniiaDama/Shutterstock.com; p. 11 Shedara Weinsberg/Shutterstock.com; p. 13 Wikipedia.com; p. 14 Sanchik/Shutterstock.com; p. 17 otsphoto/Shutterstock.com; p. 18, 20 Anna Krivitskaya/Shutterstock.com

Printed in the United States of America

CPSIA compliance information: Batch #CWNHP26: For further information contact Norwood House Press at 1-800-237-9932.

TABLE OF CONTENTS

Meet the Dachshund

Dachshunds (DAHKS-hunts) are popular pets. Dogs of this **breed** are known for their **liveliness** and their long, sausage-shaped bodies.

Some people call dachshunds "wiener dogs." The sausages we know as hot dogs were originally called dachshunds!

What Do Dachshunds Look Like?

Dachshunds are small dogs with short legs and thick, **muscular** chests.

These little dogs have a long **muzzle** and long, floppy ears. They have dark, almond-shaped eyes.

Most dachshunds have short, smooth **coats**.

Some are longhaired or **wirehaired**. A dachshund's fur is red, brown, or tan. It can be a solid color or a mix.

Dachshunds stand no more than 10 inches (25 centimeters) tall. They come in two sizes: standard and **miniature**.

Standard Dachshund

Standard dachshunds weigh up to 32 pounds (15 kilograms). Miniature dachshunds are 11 pounds (five kilograms) or less.

Where Do Dachshunds Come From?

Dachshunds come from the country of Germany. Hundreds of years ago, they were raised to help hunters. In German, their name means "badger dog."

A dachshund's bravery helped it fight fierce badgers. Its long, low body was perfect for wriggling into their underground dens. Its floppy ears kept out dirt and bugs. When it found a badger, the dog's loud bark could be heard by hunters aboveground.

Today, dachshunds are great at earthdog. It's a sport where dogs race through underground tunnels to track a **scent**.

Do Dachshunds Make Good Pets?

Dachshunds are good pets. They are smart and full of energy. They love to learn new things and play. They can live to be 20 years old!

Dachshunds are little dogs, but they sound like big dogs. They will bark loudly at strangers. They make good **watchdogs**.

What Do Dachshunds Need?

Dachshunds need exercise every day. This builds strong muscles and keeps their long backs from getting hurt.

Dachshunds are **social** dogs. They need to spend time with people.

Glossary

breed (breed): one type or kind of an animal

coats (kohts): the hair or fur that covers animals' bodies

liveliness (LIVE-lee-nuhs): being full of life and energy

miniature (MIN-ee-uh-chur): much smaller than the usual size

muscular (MUHS-kyuh-lur): having strong muscles

muzzle (MUHZ-uhl): the nose and mouth of an animal

scent (sent): a smell

social (SOH-shuhl): preferring to be around others instead of alone

watchdogs (WAHCH-dawgs): dogs kept to guard property

wirehaired (WYUR-hared): having stiff, wiry fur

Thinking Questions

1. Describe a dachshund's body.

2. What are the two sizes of dachshund?

3. What features help dachshunds hunt badgers?

4. How long can dachshunds live?

5. What helps protect a dachshund's back from injury?

Index

About the Author

Dan Lopez is a writer who loves dogs! He has a German shepherd named Hans and an Irish setter named Tam. They love to go for walks in the woods together. Sometimes, they jump in the lake for a swim. Dan lives in Indiana with his wife and three kids.